EXPLORING SCIENCE

D N A

THE MASTER MOLECULE OF LIFE

BY DARLENE R. STILLE

Content Adviser: Irwin Rubenstein, Ph.D.,
Professor Emeritus, University of Minnesota, St. Paul

Science Adviser: Terrence E. Young Jr., M.Ed., M.L.S.,
Jefferson Parish (Louisiana) Public School System

Reading Adviser: Susan Kesselring, M.A., Literacy Educator,
Rosemount-Apple Valley-Eagan (Minnesota) School District

COMPASS POINT BOOKS · MINNEAPOLIS, MINNESOTA

Compass Point Books • 3109 West 50th Street, #115 • Minneapolis, MN 55410

Visit Compass Point Books on the Internet at *www.compasspointbooks.com*
or e-mail your request to *custserv@compasspointbooks.com*

Photographs ©: Matthias Kulka/zefa/Corbis, cover, 7; Ashley Cooper/Corbis, 4; SIU/Peter Arnold, Inc., 5; Michael Abbey/Visuals Unlimited, 8 (right); Anna Clopet/Corbis, 9; Library of Congress, 10; LWA-Dann Tardif/Corbis, 12, 42; Michael A. Keller/zefa/Corbis, 14; Argus Fotoarchiv/Peter Arnold, Inc., 16; Dr. Stanley Flegler/Visuals Unlimited, 17; Photodisc, 18, 23; Digital Art/Corbis, 20; Fritz Goro/Time Life Pictures/Getty Images, 21; Hulton Archive/Getty Images, 24; Bettmann/Corbis, 25; Ed Reschke/Peter Arnold, Inc., 26; CDC/Peter Arnold, Inc., 30; NIAID/Peter Arnold, Inc., 31; Jorgen Schytte/Peter Arnold, Inc., 33; Matt Meadows/Peter Arnold, Inc., 34; SIU/Visuals Unlimited, 35; Science VU/Visuals Unlimited, 37; Stephen Jaffe/AFP/Getty Images, 39; Corbis, 40; USDA/ARS/Keith Weller, 43; H. Spichtinger/zefa/Corbis, 46.

Editor: Anthony Wacholtz
Designer/Page Production: The Design Lab
Photo Researcher: Marcie C. Spence
Illustrator: Eric Hoffmann

Art Director: Jaime Martens
Creative Director: Keith Griffin
Editorial Director: Carol Jones
Managing Editor: Catherine Neitge

Library of Congress Cataloging-in-Publication Data
Stille, Darlene R.
    DNA : the master molecule of life / by Darlene R. Stille.
       p. cm. — (Exploring science)
    Includes bibliographical references and index.
    ISBN 0-7565-1617-X (hardcover)
    1. DNA—Juvenile literature. I. Title. II. Series: Exploring science
    (Minneapolis, Minn.)
    QP624.S75 2006
    611'.018166—dc22   2005025061

    ISBN 0-7565-1762-1 (softcover)

About the Author

Darlene R. Stille is a science writer and author of more than 70 books for young people. When she was in high school, she fell in love with science. While attending the University of Illinois, she discovered that she also loved writing. She was fortunate enough to find a career as an editor and writer that allowed her to combine both of her interests. Darlene Stille now lives and writes in Michigan.

TABLE OF CONTENTS

CHAPTER ONE

The Master Molecule of Life

EMERGENCY VEHICLES with flashing lights speed down the street. Yellow tape reading "crime scene" blocks off an area around a building. Uniformed police officers keep onlookers away as a team of high-tech crime fighters arrive. They are the crime scene investigators.

Modern criminal investigators have many tools to help them solve crimes. One of the most powerful tools is the ability to collect and analyze a body chemical called deoxyribonucleic acid (DNA). DNA is in every human body cell, including hair cells, white blood cells,

Investigators search for evidence at the scene of a crime.

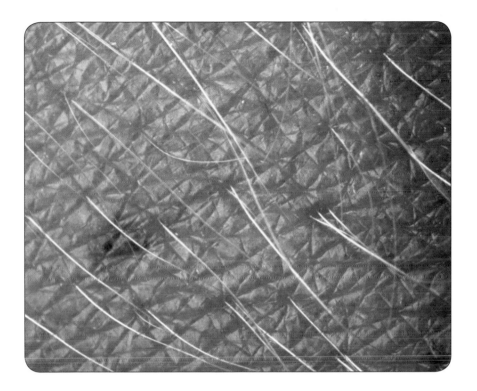

and skin cells. No two people (except identical twins) have the same DNA profile, also known as a DNA "fingerprint." Criminal investigators use this fact to help solve crimes and other mysteries.

By analyzing DNA profiles, investigators can identify individuals. They can match the DNA profile of samples from a crime scene with the DNA profile of a suspect. DNA profiles have also been used to free innocent people wrongly accused or convicted of a crime. In addition, DNA profiles can be used

The tiniest bit of skin or hair contains DNA.

DNA and the Wrongly Accused

The first person acquitted of a crime based on DNA testing was a fisherman named Kirk Bloodsworth from Maryland. He had been convicted of a crime in 1984 and was sentenced to death. In 1992, while he was on death row, a sample of Bloodsworth's DNA was compared with DNA found at the scene of the crime. The two did not match, and Bloodsworth was set free. A federal law passed in 2004 created a DNA testing program for all people facing the death penalty. A grant to help pay for the testing was named after Bloodsworth.

to identify animals. Veterinary DNA investigators can identify a lost cat or dog. DNA profiles can also help customs officials spot illegally imported endangered animal or plant species.

WHAT IS DNA, ANYWAY?

Scientists call DNA the master molecule of life. DNA is a chemical that exists in all living things. DNA is important to criminal investigators because they can identify individuals from the unique chemical composition or DNA profile of any DNA left at a crime scene. All that is needed is some hair, blood, saliva, or other cells.

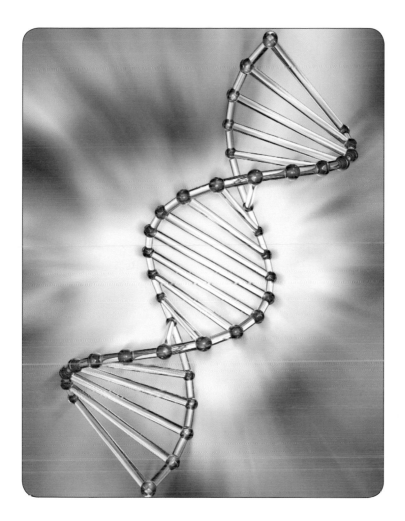

Your DNA is what makes you the individual that you are. Everyone has DNA whose chemical composition is like that of no one else. Investigators analyze DNA in special ways that can produce a unique DNA fingerprint for an individual.

DNA looks like a twisted ladder.

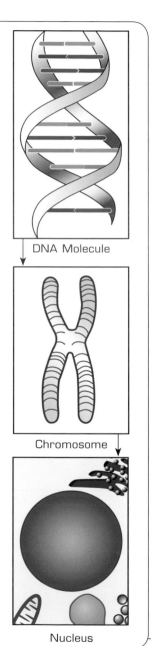

DNA Molecule

Chromosome

Nucleus

WHERE IS DNA FOUND?

There are DNA molecules in cells of every living thing on Earth. A single molecule of DNA forms each of the threadlike structures called chromosomes. Chromosomes are mostly made of DNA and another biochemical called protein. In most organisms, the chromosomes are contained in a region of the cell called the nucleus. Different species have differing numbers of chromosomes. Human beings have 46 chromosomes in each cell.

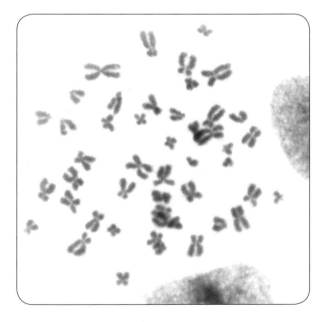

Female chromosomes are X-shaped structures found in the nucleus.

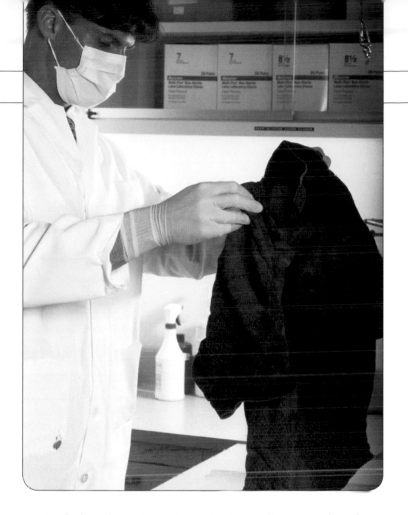

To help solve crimes, investigators collect samples of any substance that might contain DNA—skin cells, blood cells, or any other kinds of cells. They analyze the cells in a laboratory. They have ways of taking an individual's DNA apart to produce unique DNA fragments that could connect a person to the scene of a crime. To understand how DNA can be taken apart and used in this way, it is important to understand how DNA is put together and how it works. DNA is much more than just a tool for investigators.

A crime scene investigator analyzes a shirt for traces of blood, hair, or skin.

The Mystery of Russia's Royal Romanovs

Investigators use DNA profiles to solve some unusual cases. Sometimes they are successful, but other times the results are not certain. For example, investigators tried to solve an old mystery involving Russia's former royal family, the Romanovs.

Russia was in turmoil in 1917. A violent revolution overthrew the ruling czar, Nicholas II, and set up a Communist government that became known as the Soviet Union. Nicholas, his wife, Alexandra, their five children, and several others were taken prisoner and executed in July 1918.

A great mystery surrounded the fate of the Romanovs. What happened to the bodies? Did they all die? There were rumors that one of the girls, Anastasia, survived. In fact, a

The royal Romanovs pose for a family picture.

woman named Anna Anderson showed up in Berlin, Germany, in 1920 and claimed she was Anastasia.

In 1991, the Soviet Union fell. Russian and British researchers then dug up bones believed to be those of the Romanovs and conducted tests on what little DNA they could find. The tests showed that five bodies were related—a father, mother, and three daughters.

The researchers also did tests on a special kind of DNA called mitochondrial DNA.

Mitochondria are tiny structures inside cells. The job of the mitochondria is to provide energy for cells. There is a small amount of DNA in mitochondria. This DNA is inherited only from females. By analyzing the mitochondrial DNA profile, researchers can trace female ancestors back for many generations.

The mitochondrial DNA profiles showed that the mother and the three daughters were related to Prince Philip, husband of the British queen Elizabeth II. Alexandra Romanov was, in fact, the great aunt of Prince Philip.

DNA profile tests on the remains of Anna Anderson, who died in 1984, showed that she was not a Romanov. The DNA tests did not end the mystery, however. Some people questioned whether the bones really were those of the Romanovs. And where were the bones of the other two children? Even with the best DNA tests, we may never know.

Genes and DNA

ALL ANIMALS AND PLANTS, even one-celled amoebas and bacteria, have genes made of DNA. Genes carry the code for what each living organism will look like and how it will function. Children inherit their genes—and thus DNA—from their parents. Half of the child's genes come from the mother and half from the father. In reproduction, the parents' genes get mixed up. That is why children may look similar to their parents, but also different. The

A baby will look similar to his or her parents because of the traits passed on through the genes.

children's genes are a unique combination of genes from both of their parents.

WHAT IS THE DIFFERENCE BETWEEN GENES AND DNA?

The molecular form of DNA can best be thought of as a very long stringlike structure. In fact, most of our body's cells contain about 2 yards (1.8 meters) of DNA. Genes are places or regions along a strand of DNA. The DNA has a code that tells where a gene begins and where it ends.

There can be thousands of genes on one DNA strand. Researchers estimate that the DNA in a human cell contains between 20,000 and 25,000 genes. All of the genes that are contained in a species' cells are called its genome.

WHAT DO GENES DO?

Most genes direct the formation of proteins. We usually think of protein as being a category of food. We eat foods such as meat, eggs, and beans to get protein. Our bodies break down the protein molecules in our foods into smaller units called amino acids. There are 20 amino acids that become the build-

Bacon and eggs are excellent sources of protein.

DID YOU KNOW?

The scientist who discovers a new gene gets to name it. For example, an alteration in fruit flies causes little hairs to sprout on the larvae. The gene was appropriately named the "hedgehog" gene!

ing blocks of the new proteins that our body needs.

New proteins are made inside the cytoplasm, or region in the cell outside of the nucleus. Cells produce many kinds of proteins. A specific gene directs the making of a specific protein and its chemical properties. Sometimes the products of two or more genes are needed to form a protein structure for cell use.

These proteins do the work of the cell. They help the heart beat and the intestines digest food. Proteins also create skin and bones. Hemoglobin is a protein in red blood cells that carries oxygen from the lungs to every cell in the body. Proteins called enzymes make certain chemical reactions possible. Proteins called hormones direct many processes in the body, including reproduction.

The instructions for building proteins are supplied by the genes in the DNA molecule in the form of a chemical code. Just as proteins are made up of 20 smaller building blocks called amino acids, DNA is made up of four smaller building blocks called nucleotides.

Mutations: Changes in DNA

Genes can mutate, or change. The mutation begins when one of the four building blocks of the DNA is altered. These altered building blocks cause a change in the genetic coding of the new protein that is being produced.

Many things can cause a mutation. Sometimes mistakes occur when DNA reproduces itself before cell division. Certain chemicals, such as tar in cigarettes, can cause mutations. Ultraviolet rays from the sun or powerful X-rays striking DNA can cause a mutation. Scientists do not yet know all of the things that can cause mutations.

Because of the change in a gene's DNA, mutations may cause changes in proteins. Some mutations do not cause changes that can be noticed. Other mutations lead to disease by causing changes in the proteins produced. For example, some mutations in body cells can lead to cancer. Cancer cells reproduce uncontrollably to create lumps of tissue

Along with lung damage, the tar in cigarettes can cause gene mutations.

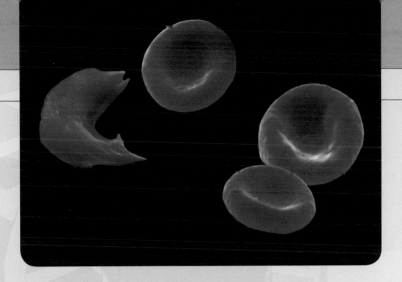

called tumors. While these mutations can be influenced by environmental circumstances, they are not directly passed along to children.

Mutations that arise in sex cells (sperm and eggs) can be passed along to children. Certain diseases result from inherited mutations. Sickle cell anemia, for example, is inherited. It comes from a mutation in a gene that codes for a protein called hemoglobin. The defective hemoglobin protein results in red blood cells that deform into the shape of a sickle. The deformed blood cells can block small blood vessels, which can cause immense pain and even death. The full extent of the disease is felt when both parents pass on a mutated gene to their child.

Other mutations are completely beneficial. A mutation in a wild grape plant, for example, gave rise to a sweeter, juicier fruit. Breeders collected seeds from the mutated grape and grew a new variety called the Concord grape.

The rough, irregular shape of sickled red blood cells can stop the flow of blood.

The Genetic Code

TO UNDERSTAND THE GENETIC CODE, it helps to think about the chemical composition of DNA as being like a language. What if you could write every book that ever existed in every language known on Earth? That feat would be amazing enough, but suppose you did all this writing using just four letters. You would have

to use short combinations of the four letters to create a kind of code for all the words that would go into those books. You would have to string together long combinations of letters to make up the words.

Something even more amazing happens in the world around us. The life of every animal, plant, and other living organism is "written" with a code that contains just four chemicals. We can think of these chemicals as being like four letters. These four chemicals (nucleotides) join together in trillions of combinations to create a long DNA molecule.

Using a four-letter alphabet to write books would be a very difficult task!

The nucleotides are distinguished by the four different chemical bases they contain. The chemical bases are adenine (A), thymine (T), cytosine (C), and guanine (G). Scientists call the nucleotides or their bases A, T, C, and G for short. The secret of the genetic code lies in how these nucleotides and their chemical bases fit together to make the DNA molecule.

A TWISTED LADDER

The DNA molecule is actually a double-stranded structure that is made up of pairs of nucleotides and resembles a long, twisted ladder. The sides of the ladder are made up of a sugar and a chemical called a phosphate. The rungs of the ladder are made up of the four chemical bases.

It takes two bases to form one rung on the DNA ladder. The two bases join in the middle of a rung. Any of the four

DNA MOLECULE

A   T
T   A
C   G
G   C

G   C
C   G
T   A
G   C

T   A
A   T
C   G

bases can be on either side of a rung. The bases, however, always pair up in the same way to make a whole rung. A always pairs up with T, and C always pairs up with G. Scientists call the two bases that make up a rung a base pair. A gene can contain thousands of base pairs.

DNA LETTERS AND WORDS

The DNA base pair pattern of a gene often codes for a given protein. The DNA also has a base pair code that signals the start and end of the gene.

When scientists analyze one of the strands of the double-stranded DNA molecule, they see nucleotide base patterns

The four colors of a DNA model represent the four nucleotide bases.

that represent the code for making a protein. A short section might look like TTTCACAAGGTTGG. For the purpose of making proteins, however, the four letters are arranged into three-letter "words." Instead of words, scientists call these three-letter units codons. Each codon directs the cell to use only one of the 20 amino acids' building blocks when it makes a protein.

MADE TO COME APART

Because the DNA is set up as a ladder, it can easily come apart. The DNA ladder "unzips" down the middle of its two-part rungs. The two sides or strands separate where the two bases join. There are two important biological reasons why this unzipping happens.

The first reason DNA comes apart is so that it can make an exact copy of itself. This allows us to grow from a single cell to the

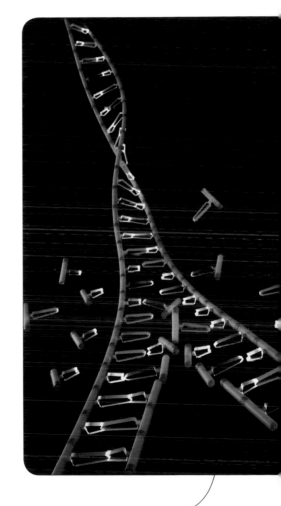

A computer-generated DNA model shows the process of unzipping.

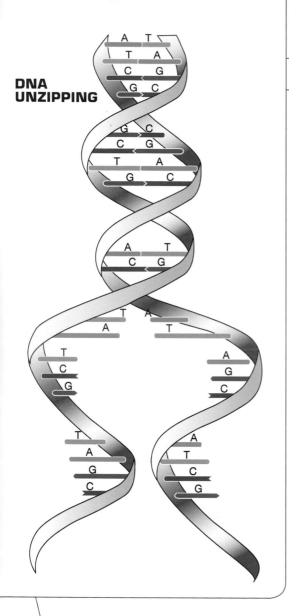

DNA UNZIPPING

billions of cells that make up a whole human being. Our bodies and all other living things grow because our cells divide and multiply. Every body cell in every living thing contains a complete copy of that organism's DNA. Before a cell divides to make two cells, the DNA must make an exact copy of itself. Having the same two bases always pair up in the same way makes this possible.

The process begins when the DNA ladder unzips down the middle of the rungs. The two strands separate where the two bases join. Each strand becomes a template, or mold, for the chemical formation of a new matching strand of DNA. New chemical bases join up with each half rung. A's join up with T's, and T's join up with A's. C's and G's join up together.

One way to think about this process is to imagine that the DNA molecule is like a photographic negative and a photographic print. One strand is the "negative" and the other strand is the "print." The negative strand can be used to make another print strand, and the print strand can be used to make another negative strand. Both of the strands contain all of the necessary information to make the other strand.

The DNA ladder also unzips so that the cell can make proteins. The whole DNA ladder does not unzip to make one protein. Only the section of DNA containing the gene for that protein unzips. Another kind of molecule called ribonucleic acid (RNA) then gets assembled on the unzipped part of the strand. The RNA directs the making of that gene's protein.

A picture and its negative are similar to the two unzipped strands of DNA.

Discovering DNA

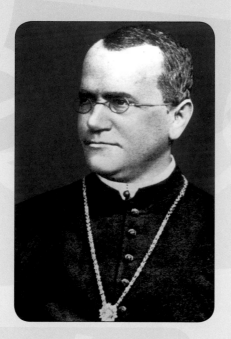

The research of many scientists helped in the discovery of DNA, what it looks like, and how it works. The idea that some factor carried genetic information from parents to offspring started with an Austrian monk named Gregor Mendel. The name *gene* was given to these factors in the early 1900s.

In 1869, a Swiss biochemist named Friedrich Miescher discovered a biochemical in cells that became known as DNA. At first, no one thought it was a very important chemical. Then researchers learned that DNA forms a major part of chromosomes. By the mid-1940s, scientists were certain that DNA was the material that passed along inherited traits. The next step was to analyze DNA and figure out how it worked.

A British chemist and molecular biologist named Rosalind Franklin used X-rays to study the structure of DNA. X-rays of

By performing experiments on pea plants in his monastery garden, Gregor Mendel originated the idea that traits get passed on over generations.

molecules can show how the atoms are arranged. Franklin and her colleague, Maurice H. Wilkins, made X-ray images that indicated important physical aspects of the DNA molecule.

Using the X-ray information, British biologist Francis Crick and American biologist James D. Watson figured out the structure of DNA in 1953. They made a model showing that DNA is shaped like a spiral ladder. Watson, Crick, and Wilkins shared the 1962 Nobel Prize for the discovery of DNA's structure. Franklin had died of cancer in 1958 and was unable to share in the award—recipients of the Nobel Prize must be alive at the time it is presented.

Professor Maurice H. Wilkins (left), Dr. Francis Crick (third from left), and Professor James D. Watson (second from right) receive the Nobel Prize.

CHAPTER FOUR

RNA and the Protein Factory

CELLS ARE LIKE tiny protein factories. An animal or plant cell has two main parts or regions called the nucleus and the cytoplasm. The DNA inside the cell nucleus does not leave the nucleus.

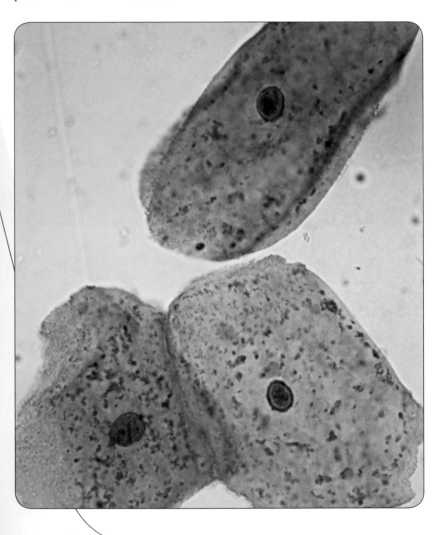

The dark spot in each of the cheek cells is the nucleus, which holds the organism's DNA.

Amino acids, the raw materials for making proteins, are in the cytoplasm. How does DNA get its instructions out of the nucleus to the rest of the cell?

DNA "talks" to the rest of the cell by using RNA, which is like a mirror image of DNA. RNA is also made up of four similar nucleotides. Three of the nucleotide bases are the same as the bases in DNA: A, C, and G. Instead of T, however, RNA has a base called uracil (U). The U base in RNA always pairs up with A.

HOW RNA IS MADE

DNA directs the synthesis, or formation of RNA inside the cell nucleus. It makes RNA on an unzipped section of the DNA molecule that equals at least one gene.

The A, C, G, and U bases of RNA pair up with the half rungs on one of the strands of the unzipped DNA ladder. An

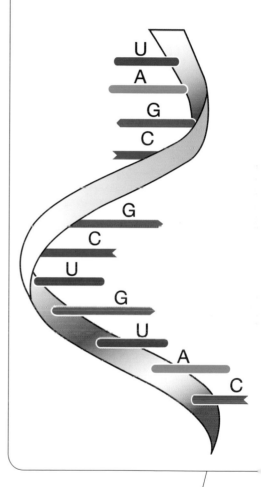

RNA MOLECULE

U
A
G
C
G
C
U
G
U
A
C

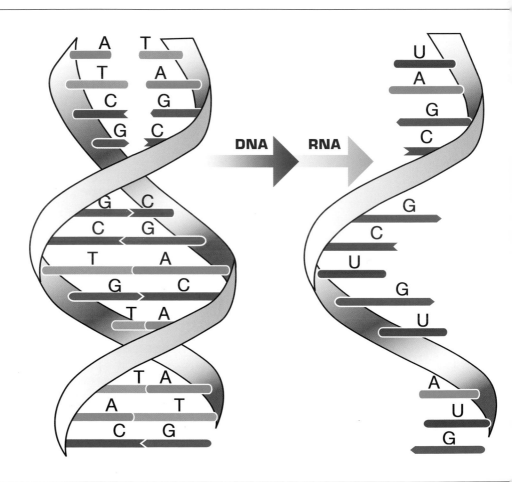

 The RNA strand matches its nucleotide bases with those on one of the strands of DNA.

RNA molecule, however, does not have two strands and does not form a twisted double-stranded ladder. Instead, a single strand of RNA moves out of the cell nucleus and into the surrounding cytoplasm.

HOW RNA WORKS

There are different kinds of RNA that do different jobs. Messenger RNA (mRNA) carries the message coded in the DNA. It heads for a structure in the cell cytoplasm called a ribosome. Ribosomes are like workbenches in the cell. Proteins get made on this ribosome workbench.

A kind of RNA called transfer RNA (tRNA) gathers up each of the amino acids needed to make a protein. There is at least one tRNA for each amino acid. Meanwhile, the ribosome starts to read a strand of mRNA. Each three-letter RNA codon calls for a different tRNA joined to its amino acid. The ribosome, using the codon directions contained in the mRNA, builds a protein one amino acid at a time. The ribosome moves along the mRNA, adding amino acids until it comes to a "stop signal." The stop signal is a specific sequence of bases in the mRNA that ends the addition of amino acids. The completed protein then leaves the ribosome.

DID YOU KNOW?

Animals make proteins from amino acids that they get from protein in foods. Plants make proteins from sugar, nitrogen, sulfur, and phosphorus. Plants make sugar using water, the energy in sunlight, and carbon dioxide from the air. Plant roots absorb minerals from the soil.

RNA Viruses

Are the traits of every organism always passed along in DNA? The only "living thing" that does not pass along its genetic information in DNA is a kind of virus called an RNA virus. RNA viruses cause many common infections, such as colds and the flu.

It is hard to say whether any kind of virus is really a living thing. Viruses do not behave like living things until they infect the cells of an organism. A virus is made of genetic material, either DNA or RNA, inside a protein shell or coat. Once inside a cell, a virus sheds its coat and turns its genes loose. Since a virus cannot reproduce on its own, its genes take over the host cell and command it to make more viruses.

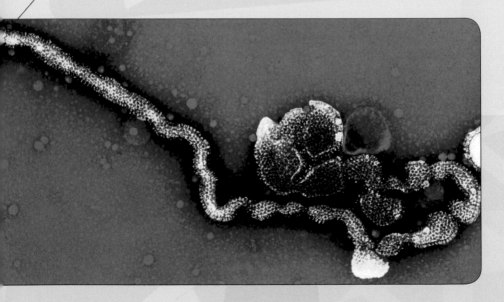

Although this strand of Influenza type C does not cause epidemics, types A and B can spread quickly.

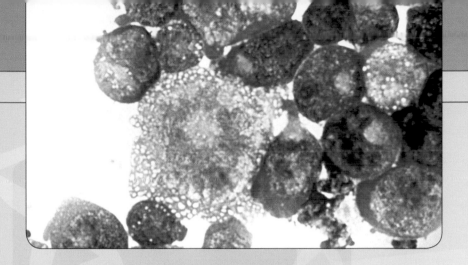

RNA viruses mutate, or change, rapidly. The mutations help them outsmart the body's defense system. It is difficult to make vaccines that protect against RNA viruses. Drug companies must make new flu vaccines almost every year because the flu virus's RNA changes so rapidly.

RNA retroviruses are even more strange. When a retrovirus invades a cell, it turns its RNA loose. The RNA serves as a template for making a DNA copy. The viral DNA then goes into the DNA of the cell and directs the building of viral proteins. This is just the reverse of what usually happens, and that is where the retrovirus gets its name. Literally, a retrovirus is a "backward virus."

Some very dangerous viruses are retroviruses. HIV, the virus that causes AIDS by infecting immune system cells, is a retrovirus. However, retroviruses can also be used in gene therapy to cure human diseases. A normal gene could be inserted into the retrovirus. When the retrovirus inserts its genes into the DNA of a cell, it would carry the normal gene along. Scientist must first make sure that they can make this technique work and that they use a harmless retrovirus.

HIV wreaks havoc on a number of cells.

Making Use of DNA

ONCE SCIENTISTS HAD LEARNED about DNA, they found many ways to employ this master molecule. They use a method called genetic engineering to take genes from one species and put them into a different species. They can make "maps" of genes and where they are located on chromosomes. They can make DNA fingerprints of an individual that can be used to catch criminals, identify bodies, and solve other kinds of mysteries.

GENETIC ENGINEERING

Genetic engineering is making changes to the genes in a plant, animal, or other organism. The changes involve taking a gene from one organism and putting it into another organism. The gene can even come from another species.

For example, scientists can take a gene from the DNA of an animal and put it into the DNA of a plant, which would then be called a transgenic plant. Scientists create transgenic plants for a number of reasons. Some transgenic plants resist insects and other pests. Some crop plants could be created that would not be harmed by weed

DID YOU KNOW?

Genetic engineering is also called recombinant DNA technology and gene splicing.

killers or that wouldn't require large amounts of chemical pesticides.

To remove and insert genes, scientists use "chemical scissors" and "chemical glue." Certain chemicals called enzymes

Genetic research is conducted all over the world. Genetic engineers perform a variety of tests in a busy laboratory in Egypt.

can cut or break a DNA molecule. Scientists use many kinds of chemical scissors. Each chemical cuts a DNA molecule at different places according to the different group of bases present at a cut site.

A scientist uses a gene gun to shoot DNA fragments into the nucleus of plant cells.

GENETICALLY ENGINEERED PRODUCTS

Some drugs are now made by genetic engineering. The first genetically engineered drug was human insulin. Insulin is a hormone that helps remove sugar from the blood. The bodies of people with Type I diabetes do not produce insulin. They must take insulin injections. Scientists "glued" the human insulin gene into the DNA of a bacterium, a microscopic organism. The bacteria became microscopic drug factories that produce this important protein.

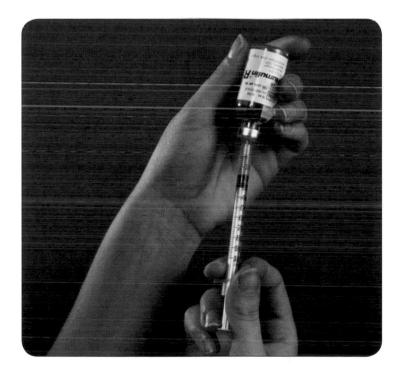

Human insulin made using recombinant DNA is used to control diabetes.

Scientists have also genetically engineered plants to resist pests and diseases. They are working on making genetically engineered plants and animals that are bigger, better tasting, and more nutritious.

DNA FINGERPRINTING

Chemical scissors proved to be very useful in creating accurate DNA fingerprints, or profiles, that represent DNA patterns unique to an individual. Scientists begin by using enzymes to cut the microscopic strands of DNA into different fragments.

Next the scientists put a solution containing the fragments of DNA onto a gelatinlike substance called a gel. Then they run an electric current through the gel. The electric current pulls the fragments of DNA into different positions on the gel. This technique is called electrophoresis. The DNA fragments separate into many bands or strips because of their different lengths. The smaller the fragment is, the faster it moves in the gel.

Finally the scientists take a picture of the DNA bands. The picture shows a pattern of bands on the film that looks a little like a bar code. The band pattern is different for each individual. This band pattern is the DNA fingerprint or profile.

Another kind of DNA fingerprinting called the PCR test unzips the DNA molecule and uses a chemical to make many copies of the DNA. Investigators then look for a particular

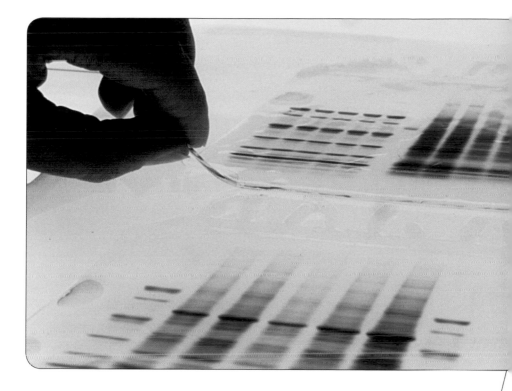

form of a gene. They compare the gene in the DNA sample with all known forms of the gene. Odds range from 1 in 100,000 to 1 in 1 million that the form of the gene in the crime scene sample does not belong to the suspect. If need be, several genes can be tested in this way to rule out a suspect.

PCR fingerprinting is fast and relatively inexpensive, but it is usually not as accurate as gel analysis of the DNA bands. On the other hand, it only requires a very small amount of the DNA for the test.

DNA bands are shown by using gel electrophoresis.

DNA SEQUENCING

A major goal of geneticists, scientists who study genes, was to sequence the base pair order of the complete human genome. They wanted to determine the order of all the base pairs that make up the entire set of instructions carried in human DNA. A huge international project, called the Human Genome Project, began in 1990.

These scientists used many high-tech methods. They cut up DNA into fragments of different lengths with chemical scissors. They used special machines to read the sequence of DNA bases in the fragments. Then they put all the base sequence information in all the different fragments together. By 2003, they had sequenced all of the 3 billion bases in the entire human genome.

This information was put into computer databases. Now scientists all over the world are studying each gene to determine the protein or start/stop signal it codes for. They also

DID YOU KNOW?

In addition to the human genome, scientists have also sequenced the DNA in other organisms, including the mouse, the rat, two kinds of fruit flies, yeast, some roundworms, many microbes, a mustard weed, and rice.

want to learn what happens when a gene is defective. How can
a defect in a given gene cause a specific disease?

Dr. Robert Waterston of the University of Washington Genome
Center displays the development of human genome sequencing.

GENETIC MEDICINE

Doctors believe that genetic science will revolutionize medicine. A newborn could have a DNA sequence profile made of its genes. This profile would tell what diseases the person might get later in life. Steps could be taken to help prevent the

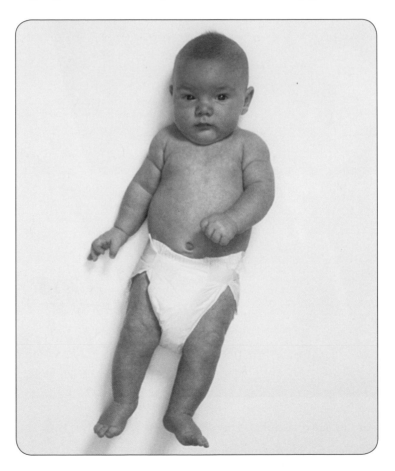

Genetic scientists may be able to map out an individual's chance for inheriting diseases at the time he or she is a baby.

disease. For example, a person with a gene that causes suscep-
tibility to skin cancer could avoid sunburn, which could cause
further damage to DNA.

Genetic scientists also want to treat inherited diseases
with gene therapy. They want to cure these diseases with
genetic engineering. They want to replace defective genes with
normal ones that code for the correct protein.

ETHICS AND SAFETY

Many people are concerned about ethical and safety issues
involving DNA. Some people believe that genetic engineering
is wrong. They do not think that scientists should insert genes
from one species into another.

Other people are concerned about the safety of genetically
engineered drugs, foods, and other products. Could genetic
engineering accidentally create a harmful microorganism,
such as a bacterium? Could genetically engineered foods cause
allergic reactions in some people?

Many people wonder how genetic information will be
used. Could genetic profiles lead to a new form of discrimi-
nation? Will employers refuse to hire people with certain
defective genes? Will insurance companies refuse to sell such
individuals insurance policies?

Still others wonder if people want to know what diseases

may be coded for in their genes. Should a person be told he or she may have a genetic disease for which there is no cure?

The promise of DNA technology is great, but the scientific advances raise many questions. Ethics and safety are issues that will need the attention of everyone, from scientists and government officials to ordinary citizens. All citizens need to understand what DNA is and how DNA technology is used. Then they will be able to make good decisions about ethics, safety, and their health.

A person may not want to know of an incurable genetic disease he or she may develop later in life.

Jobs in Genetics or Careers with DNA

DNA technology has resulted in many new kinds of careers. Many careers involve basic research. Some molecular biologists study the DNA sequences that make up genes. They want to know why some genes are "turned on" in some cells and not others. Biochemists study the chemical reactions involving proteins that are coded for by DNA. Geneticists study how specific parts of the DNA molecule pass traits from parents to offspring. They are especially interested in genes involved in inherited diseases. Many of these researchers use information gathered by the Human Genome Project to try to discover what protein each gene codes for and how that protein acts in the body.

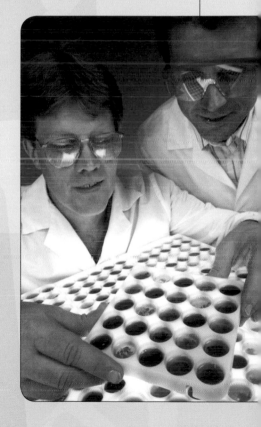

People in other careers apply the lessons learned from basic research. Virologists study the genes of viruses and how they might be used to make vaccines or to treat diseases caused by viruses. Cancer specialists study how genes are involved in creating tumors and

Biochemists analyze hybrid corn samples in a laboratory.

look for ways to correct these defective genes. Drug research-ers and other biotechnologists use genetic engineering to produce better medicines and other products. Many kinds of medical scientists are working on ways to use gene therapy to treat or cure disease. Some work with virologists to find harm-less viruses that could "infect" a person with a healthy gene.

There are also careers related to genetics that are not involved in research. For example, genetic counselors are indi-viduals trained in human genetics who help people cope with genetic information. Along with psychologists and social work-ers, genetic counselors help couples that learn they might be carrying a disease gene that could be passed on to children. In the future, genetic counselors will help people learn how to deal with information about their genetic profiles.

Genetics plays an increasing role in other fields. Some law-yers, for example, specialize in getting patents for substances made with biotechnology. Trial lawyers must understand the basics of DNA profiling in order to prosecute or defend people accused of a crime.

There are even historians and anthropologists who spe-cialize in using DNA as a tool. By analyzing bits of DNA from ancient people, plants, and animals, these scientists are learn-ing to trace the relationships to present-day people, plants, and animals.

amino acids—building blocks of proteins

bases—four basic chemicals that form the rungs of the DNA ladder

base pair—two joined DNA bases, either A to T or C to G

chromosomes—threadlike structures in the nucleus that carry the genes

codons—three-base units that code for an amino acid

cytoplasm—part of the cell outside of the nucleus

DNA (deoxyribonucleic acid)—the molecule of which genes are made

DNA sequencing—determining the exact order of the base pairs in a segment of DNA

electrophoresis—the use of an electric current to separate and sort different-length pieces of DNA in a gel

genes—the basic units of heredity

gene therapy—inserting normal genes to take over the job of defective genes that had caused disease

genetic engineering—inserting genes from one organism into the chromosomes of another organism

genetic profiles—listings of a person's genes, especially those that could lead to disease

genome—all of the genes contained in the cells of a specific species

mutation—a change resulting in a new biological trait or characteristic

nucleus—the command center of the cell that gives instructions to the other parts of the cell

protein—molecule composed of amino acids. It is made by animal and plant cells to carry out various functions

retrovirus—an RNA virus that can insert its genes into the DNA of a cell

ribosome—structure that helps assemble amino acids into proteins

RNA (ribonucleic acid)—a molecule used to assemble proteins and carry out other cellular functions

▸ Scientists have developed DNA microchips that contain a gene cut up into tiny pieces and placed inside squares. To check for mutations in a copy of the gene, samples of cellular RNA stained with a glowing dye are placed on the chip. If the glowing RNA fails to stick to any section of the microchip, there might be a mutation in that part of the gene.

▸ American biologist Barbara McClintock used experiments with corn to prove that pieces of DNA can jump from one place on a chromosome to another. These jumping genes, or transposons, might move in response to changes in an organism's environment.

▸ The four bases of DNA can be arranged into 64 three-base codons. There are only 20 amino acids, so several codons code for the same amino acid.

▸ James Watson, one of the scientists who discovered the structure of DNA in the 1950s, headed the Human Genome Project from 1990 to 1992.

▸ DNA is in the nucleus of every living thing except bacteria and blue-green algae. These organisms do not have a nucleus.

▸ PCR (polymerase chain reaction) is a technique that makes many copies of a piece of DNA quickly and inexpensively. Even if only a tiny bit of DNA is available in a sample, PCR can make many copies so that the DNA can be analyzed.

▸ Mice and humans share about 99 percent of the same DNA. Because there is only about 1 percent difference, it is possible to study genes in mice to find out how they work in humans.

▸ DNA strands are so thin that they can only be seen when the chromosomes coil up before a cell begins to divide. Even then, the chromosomes can only be seen with powerful microscopes.

▸ Gene maps can help medical researchers hunt for genes involved in disease. The researchers usually study diseases that run in families. By making gene maps, researchers have found the locations on chromosomes of genes involved in many diseases, including cystic fibrosis, muscular dystrophy, and Huntington's disease.

The DNA of humans and mice is astonishingly similar.

At the Library

De la Bedoyere, Camilla. *The Discovery of DNA*. Milwaukee: World Almanac Library, 2005.

Fridell, Ron. *DNA Fingerprinting: The Ultimate Identity*. New York: Franklin Watts/Scholastic, 2001.

Hamilton, Janet. *James Watson: Solving the Mystery of DNA*. Berkeley Heights, NJ: Enslow Publishers, 2004.

Walker, Richard. *Genes and DNA*. Boston: Kingfisher, 2003.

On the Web

For more information on **DNA,** use FactHound to track down Web sites related to this book.

1. Go to *www.facthound.com*
2. Type in a search word related to this book or this book ID: **075651617X**
3. Click on the *Fetch It* button.

FactHound will find the best Web sites for you.

On the Road

DNA EpiCenter
33 Gallows Lane
New London, CT 06320
860/442-0391

Diving into the Gene Pool
The Exploratorium
3601 Lyon St.
San Francisco, CA 94123
415/EXP-LORE

Explore all the books in this series:

Animal Cells: Smallest Units of Life
ISBN: 0-7565-1616-1

Chemical Change: From Fireworks to Rust
ISBN: 0-7565-1256-5

DNA: The Master Molecule of Life
ISBN: 0-7565-1617-X

Erosion: How Land Forms, How It Changes
ISBN: 0-7565-0854-1

Genetics: A Living Blueprint
ISBN: 0-7565-1618-8

Manipulating Light: Reflection, Refraction, and Absorption
ISBN: 0-7565-1258-1

Minerals: From Apatite to Zinc
ISBN: 0-7565-0855-X

Natural Resources: Using and Protecting Earth's Supplies
ISBN: 0-7565-0856-8

Physical Change: Reshaping Matter
ISBN: 0-7565-1257-3

Plant Cells: The Building Blocks of Plants
ISBN: 0-7565-1619-6

Soil: Digging Into Earth's Vital Resources
ISBN: 0-7565-0857-6

Waves: Energy on the Move
ISBN: 0-7565-1259-X